D1716224

NERF BLASTERS

BY NATHAN SOMMER

BELLWETHER MEDIA · MINNEAPOLIS, MN

EPIC

Action and adventure collide in **EPIC**. Plunge into a universe of powerful beasts, hair-raising tales, and high-speed excitement. Astonishing explorations await. Can you handle it?

This edition first published in 2022 by Bellwether Media, Inc.

Library of Congress Cataloging-in-Publication Data
Names: Sommer, Nathan, author.
Title: Nerf Blasters / by Nathan Sommer.
Description: Minneapolis, MN : Bellwether Media, Inc., 2022. | Series: Epic
  : Favorite toys | Includes bibliographical references and index. |
  Audience: Ages 7-12 | Audience: Grades 2-3 | Summary: "Engaging images
  accompany information about Nerf blasters. The combination of
  high-interest subject matter and light text is intended for students in
  grades 2 through 7"–Provided by publisher.
Identifiers: LCCN 2021044268 (print) | LCCN 2021044269 (ebook) | ISBN
  9781644876374 (library binding) | ISBN 9781648346484 (ebook)
Subjects: LCSH: NERF toys–Juvenile literature.
Classification: LCC GV1220.9 .S66 2022 (print) | LCC GV1220.9 (ebook) |
  DDC 688.7/2–dc23
LC record available at https://lccn.loc.gov/2021044268
LC ebook record available at https://lccn.loc.gov/2021044269

Editor: Elizabeth Neuenfeldt   Designer: Josh Brink

Printed in the United States of America, North Mankato, MN.

TABLE OF CONTENTS

Family Nerf Battle

A family plays outside with their Nerf blasters. **Darts** fly through the air.

Suddenly, a boy leaps up from a bush. He hits his mother in one shot. He wins this Nerf battle!

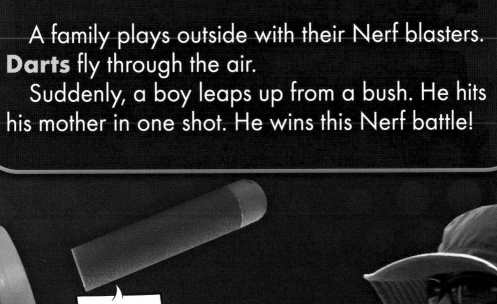

DART

The History of Nerf Blasters

Reyn Guyer **invented** Nerf balls in 1969. These **foam** balls let kids safely play indoors. More than 4.5 million Nerf balls were sold in 1969! Soon, Nerf footballs and basketball games were made.

A BUSY TOY MAKER

REYN GUYER ALSO CREATED THE BOARD GAME *TWISTER*. HE IS IN HASBRO'S INVENTORS HALL OF FAME!

NERF BLASTER BEGINNINGS

**Reyn Guyer's Hometown,
Saint Paul, Minnesota = ⬤**

NERF BALL

BLAST-A-BALL

The first Nerf blaster **debuted** in 1989. It was called the Blast-a-Ball. The blaster fired one Nerf ball per shot. Users could fire balls up to 40 feet (12 meters)!

Other early Nerf blasters shot foam arrows and **missiles**. The Bow 'n' Arrow fired long arrows. They were nearly 1 foot (0.3 meters) long!

BOW 'N' ARROW

A LOT OF DARTS

MORE THAN 4 BILLION NERF DARTS HAVE BEEN MADE SINCE 1992.

In 1992, the Sharpshooter was made. It used foam darts.

Dart blasters quickly became popular. In 2003, N-Strike blasters used darts with rubber tips. More kinds of darts were made, too. Some darts **whistled** in the air. Others glowed in the dark!

N-STRIKE ELITE HYPERFIRE BLASTER

NERF BLASTER TIMELINE

1969
Reyn Guyer invents the Nerf ball

1989
The first Nerf blaster is released

1992
The first Nerf blaster to use darts is sold in stores

2003
The first N-Strike blaster is released

2016
The first remote-controlled blaster debuts

RUBBER TIP

Nerf Blasters Today

There are many types of Nerf blasters today. Nerf Ultra blasters shoot darts 120 feet (37 meters)!

The TerraScout is a **drone**. It uses a camera and remote for sneak attacks!

NERF BLASTER TYPES

Nerf Elite 2.0

Nerf DinoSquad

Nerf *Fortnite*

**Nerf
Super Soaker**

RIVAL
BLASTER

Rival blasters are made for teenagers and adults. They can fire balls at nearly 70 miles (113 kilometers) per hour!

Other blasters are based on movies and video games. Star Wars and *Fortnite* blasters are popular **collectibles**.

NERF DOG

• • • • • • • • • • • • •

NERF DOG TOYS WERE FIRST MADE IN 2013. THE TENNIS BALL BLASTER SHOOTS BALLS 50 FEET (15 METERS)!

FORTNITE BLASTER

17

More Than A Toy

Nerf fans attend Nerf Challenge. They battle on **obstacle courses** and try out new toys. Fans also meet for giant Nerf battles. In 2016, 2,289 people met to battle!

NERF CHALLENGE

JARED'S EPIC BLASTER BATTLE PROFILE

What Is It? The world's largest Nerf battle

When Did It Begin? 2016

Where Is It?
AT&T Stadium in Arlington, Texas

When Does It Happen?
Once a year

Nerf blasters are fun online, too. Gamers play *NERF Strike* on **Roblox**. Nerf battles are also held on the *NERF Epic Pranks!* **app**.

NERF STRIKE ON ROBLOX

Nerf blasters and games are fun for people of all ages!

Glossary

app—a program or game that can be downloaded onto mobile devices

collectibles—items that are seen as valuable

darts—thin foam pieces fired out of Nerf blasters

debuted—was shown to the public for the first time

drone—a remote-controlled device that uses cameras to get around

foam—a soft, squishy material

invented—made something for the first time

missiles—short, round pieces with fins that are fired out of some Nerf blasters

obstacle courses—paths with added challenges along the way

Roblox—a website and app where people can play games created by other users

whistled—made a loud, high-pitched noise

To Learn More

AT THE LIBRARY

Bowman, Chris. *Lego Bricks*. Minneapolis, Minn.: Bellwether Media, 2022.

Hasbro U.K. *Nerf Ultimate Activity Handbook*. London, U.K.: Hachette Children's Group, 2018.

Thomas, Rachael L. *Nerf Genius: Reyn Guyer*. Minneapolis, Minn.: Abdo Publishing, 2019.

ON THE WEB

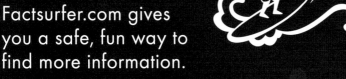

FACTSURFER

Factsurfer.com gives you a safe, fun way to find more information.

1. Go to www.factsurfer.com.

2. Enter "Nerf blasters" into the search box and click 🔍.

3. Select your book cover to see a list of related content.

Index